Science and Technology

Handheld Gadgets

Neil Morris

Raintree

Chicago, Illinois

www.heinemannraintree.com
Visit our website to find out more information about Heinemann-Raintree books.

To order:
☎ Phone 888-454-2279
🖥 Visit www.heinemannraintree.com to browse our catalog and order online.

Edited by Andrew Farrow, Adam Miller, and Diyan Leake
Designed by Victoria Allen
Original illustrations © Capstone Global Library Ltd 2012
Illustrated by Oxford Designers and Illustrators
Picture research by Elizabeth Alexander
Originated by Capstone Global Library Ltd
Printed and bound in China by CTPS

15 14 13 12 11
10 9 8 7 6 5 4 3 2 1

Library of Congress Cataloging-in-Publication Data
Morris, Neil, 1946-
　Handheld gadgets / Neil Morris.
　　p. cm.—(Sci-hi. Science and technology)
　Includes bibliographical references and index.
　ISBN 978-1-4109-4276-0 (hc)—ISBN 978-1-4109-4285-2 (pb) 1. Miniature electronic equipment—Juvenile literature. 2. Household electronics—Juvenile literature. I. Title.
　TK7880.G73 2012
　621.381—dc22　　　　　　2010054331

Acknowledgments
The author and publishers are grateful to the following for permission to reproduce copyright material: Alamy pp. **4** bottom (© Ianni Dimitrov), **16** (© Stacy Walsh Rosenstock), **30** (© Ian Shaw), **33** (© Ojo Images Ltd), **39** (© 67photo), **40** (© Synthetic Alan King); Corbis pp. 12 (© J. L. Cereijido/epa), **27** (© HO/Reuters), **35** (© Tim Pannell), **37** (© Eddie Keogh/Reuters); © Corbis p. **20**; Getty Images pp. **8** (Barbara Sax/AFP), **11** (Jason Alden/Bloomberg), **14** (Sankei); gps.gov p. **22**; iStockphoto p. **34** (© Simon Podgorsek); Rex Features p. **38** (Matti Bjorkman); Science Photo Library p. **36** (Ian Hooton); Shutterstock pp. **4** top (© sextoacto), **6** (© Eduard Stelmakh), **9** (© Theodore Scott), **10** (© Chris Baynham), **15** (© Dino O.), **17** (© DMSU), **18** (© Gemenacom), **19** (© Peter Grosch), **21** (© Pincasso), **25** (© Alberto Zornetta), **26** (© Phil Date), **28** (© AVAVA), **32** (© Eduardo Rivero), **contents page** top (© Peter Grosch), **contents page** bottom (© Eduardo Rivero), **all background and design features**; SSPL p. **24** (© Science Museum); Thoroughbred Ford/Ford p. **41**.

Main cover photograph of a smartphone, reproduced with permission of Getty Images (Bloomberg); inset cover photograph of a brain reproduced with permission of shutterstock (© Lukiyanova Natalia/frenta).

The publisher would like to thank literary consultant Nancy Harris and content consultant Suzy Gazlay for their assistance in the preparation of this book.

Contents

Some words are shown in bold, **like this**. These words are explained in the glossary. You will find important information and definitions underlined, <u>like this</u>.

What is e-waste?

Turn to page 19 to find out!

What do megapixels do?

Find out on page 32!

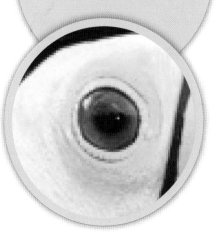

The Whole World in Your Hands

Gadgets are small devices that we find useful. In this book we will look at some gadgets that are small enough to hold in our hands. This makes them even more useful, because we can use them on the move.

Handheld gadgets are getting smaller and more powerful all the time. Look at cell phones, for example. Modern **smartphones** are cell phones that are tiny computers. They take photos and make videos. Many of them can communicate through the Internet (see page 9) and do many other things, too.

Unplugged

Gadgets need to be totally **portable**. This means you can hold them in your hand and move around as much as you want. Most use batteries you can recharge (refill the power for). That's the difference between a desktop computer and a laptop, or between a landline phone and a cell phone.

Smartphones can take photos and send them to other phones.

How electronic gadgets work

Electronic gadgets work with the help of small **components** (parts), such as **microchips** and **transistors**. These components control and direct tiny amounts of electricity. Scientists have gradually made them smaller, lighter, and more powerful. When we press a key or a button to write a text message or take a photo, the electronic component turns our action into a stream of numbers. This is a kind of code. The gadget either stores the numbers, or it sends the code to another device. The new device receives the signal. It turns the code back into the original text or photo.

Waves of energy

Electronic gadgets use **energy** (power) to communicate with each other. These rays of energy come originally from the Sun. The rays of energy are called **electromagnetic radiation**. They travel in waves (see the diagram on the right). Handheld gadgets use waves of energy called **radio waves** to communicate with each other.

*This diagram shows the range of electromagnetic waves. The low-**frequency** waves have the least energy. The high-frequency ones have the most.*

E-GADGETS

We also use the word *electronic* to refer to anything that involves the use of a computer. This is what the "e-" stands for when we send email or read an e-book on an e-reader.

low frequency

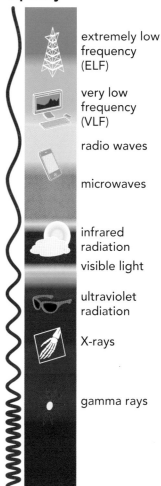

extremely low frequency (ELF)

very low frequency (VLF)

radio waves

microwaves

infrared radiation

visible light

ultraviolet radiation

X-rays

gamma rays

high frequency

COMPUTERS

Home computers were introduced in the late 1970s. They were originally desktop machines. As use of the Internet grew, people wanted to be able to move around with their personal computer. This led to portable versions with rechargeable batteries. The screen folded out from the keyboard. Eventually, smaller versions had **touchscreens**.

Laptops

Laptops are small and light enough to sit on a user's lap. Smaller versions are often called notebooks. A laptop's battery recharges when it is plugged into a wall socket. It can power the computer for several hours. In addition to a display and a keyboard, a laptop has a **touchpad** that does the same job as a computer **mouse**. Laptops have become very popular in recent years. Many people use them instead of a desktop computer.

The battery and clear screen of a modern laptop mean that it can be used anywhere.

PERSONAL ORGANIZERS

Many people like to keep an up-to-date calendar and address book in one place. Before computers became small enough to be portable, paper booklets were kept in leather wallets to form personal organizers. Other pieces of stationery could also be kept in the same place. These are still popular with some users, but electronic personal organizers, or **digital assistants**, have replaced most paper versions.

PDAs

A personal digital assistant (PDA) is sometimes called a palmtop computer. This is because it is small enough to be held in the palm of the hand. PDAs first appeared in the 1990s. They had the same features as earlier paper versions. They had a calendar, an address book, and a program for creating the text (or words) of memos and other notes.

In recent PDA models, small keyboards have been replaced by touchscreens. PDA programs allow users to transfer **data** (information) to another computer, for **backup** (extra copies) and security. Since 1993 smartphones have taken over from PDAs, because they do all of these things and more. Developments in technology mean that new, smaller gadgets can do much more than old, larger ones.

Tablet computers and the Internet

Tablets (**tablet computers**) are small computers with a touchscreen. Apple launched its iPad in April 2010 in the United States. They sold 3 million iPads in 80 days. Wireless connection to the Internet is very important for these devices. It allows users to browse the **World Wide Web** (see opposite), send and receive email, and play games using their tablet computer.

WHO DID THAT?
APPLE MAN

In 1974 a 19-year-old computer technician named Steve Jobs began working on new programs for video games in California. In 1976 he founded a computer company called Apple with two other people. By 1981 the company had sales of $335 million. By 2009 Apple's sales were more than 100 times greater than that, and Steve Jobs was still its boss. He has invented or helped invent many things used in computing.

This tablet computer uses software to turn the screen into a musical keyboard.

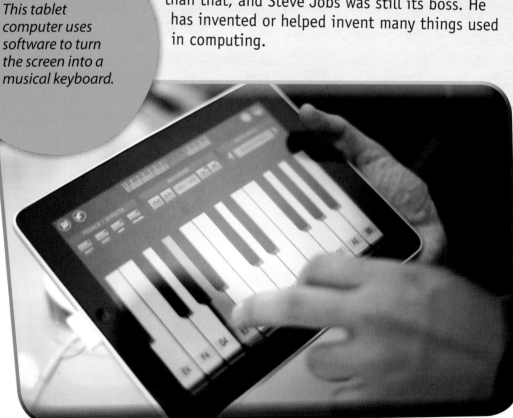

What is the Internet?

<u>The Internet is a huge network of computers</u>. It links millions of computers around the world. No one owns the Internet. A nonprofit organization called the Internet Society watches over it. Individuals connect to the network through companies called **service providers**, which allow them to use the World Wide Web. The World Wide Web is a set of documents contained in pages and websites (groups of pages). These are connected by electronic words or pictures called **hyperlinks**. Computers use **software** called **browsers** to search and move around the Web.

BRIGHT IDEA: INVENTING THE WORLD WIDE WEB

British scientist Sir Timothy Berners-Lee invented the World Wide Web in 1990. He created the first website for CERN, a scientific organization in Switzerland. Over the next 20 years, the Web grew enormously. In 2008 Berners-Lee established the World Wide Web Foundation. The foundation aims to expand the Web and keep it free to use and open to everyone. In 2010 experts figured out that the Web contained nearly 15 billion pages.

This is what a portable computer looked like in the 1980s, before the Internet existed.

Wireless networks

Portable computers use a wireless network, sometimes called **Wi-Fi**, to connect to the Internet. The network sends information along wires to a device called a **router**. The router turns the information into radio waves. A computer within its range can pick up these signals. Each Wi-Fi area is called a **hotspot**. The number of free-to-use hotspots in libraries, stores, and cafés is increasing.

The touchpad on this laptop can also be used to control the cursor instead of a mouse.

touchpad

FROM QWERTY TO MOUSEY

Some handheld computers have a keyboard with the traditional QWERTY layout. It is named after the order of the first six letters in the top row. This system was introduced to typewriters in 1872. The mouse is another common handheld gadget. This pointing device moves a **cursor** (pointer) around the screen and is used for inputting commands.

Touchscreen technology

Touchscreens are perfect for portable computers, because they do away with the separate keyboard. Instead, the traditional QWERTY layout appears on the screen. <u>One of the most common touchscreen technologies works by storing electricity. The stored electricity is harmless. It is called an electrical **charge**.</u>

When you touch the screen with your finger, some of the charge moves to you. Then there is less charge on the screen. The drop in charge is measured at each corner of the screen. This allows the computer to calculate the exact position of the touch.

The touchscreen layout of letters on this tablet is the same as on a physical keyboard.

VIRUSES

<u>A computer virus is a program that can spread from one device to another by making copies of itself.</u> Viruses can damage or destroy a computer's information. If a virus is attached to an email and sent to a computer, it can infect the computer when the **attachment** (file added) is opened. Many viruses can be found by anti-virus software, which allows you to destroy them before they damage your computer.

PHONES

Cell phones are the most popular handheld gadgets of the 21st century. In 1990, when cell phones were still new, there were 12 million cell phone users around the world. By 2010 there were about 4.6 billion cell phones in use. This was enough for one cell phone for more than two-thirds of the world's population.

From walkie-talkies to cell phones

In 1943 a Canadian inventor named Donald Hings developed a phone that used radio waves. It did not need to be plugged into the wall. People could use it to have a two-way conversation. It became known as a **walkie-talkie**. Walkie-talkies were hugely successful.

A U.S. telecommunications expert named Martin Cooper made the first public cell phone call in New York in 1973. His phone weighed 1 kilogram (2.2 pounds). Modern cells weigh less than one-tenth of that. It was another 10 years before cell phone service could be purchased. Early cell phones cost the equivalent of more than $7,500 today!

Martin Cooper holds up one of his early handsets. It came to be known as the "brick phone"!

Cell phones and cells

Cell phones are telephones that use radio waves to send the signal. When you make a call, a device called a **receiver** picks up the radio signal from your phone. It sends the signal on to another receiver, and so on, until it reaches a device called a **transmitter** near the person you are calling. The transmitter sends out signals to cell phones. The receivers and transmitters are called **base stations**. Each station covers an area of about 26 square kilometers (10 square miles). This area is called a **cell**.

Your cell phone uses a built-in **antenna**. This is a device that sends and receives radio signals. When you are near the edge of a base station's cell, your phone's signal strength gets weaker. In a far-off area, you might have no signal at all.

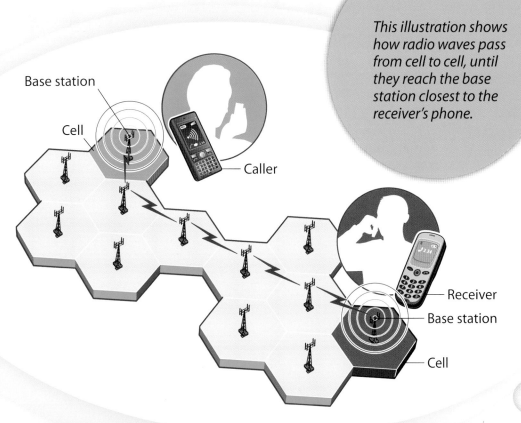

This illustration shows how radio waves pass from cell to cell, until they reach the base station closest to the receiver's phone.

Base station

Cell

Caller

Receiver

Base station

Cell

13

Smartphones

A smartphone does a lot more than make and take calls. It is really a handheld computer. You can use a smartphone to:

access the Internet

send and receive phone calls and messages

send and receive email

find your position and the way to other places using information from satellites and maps

read e-books (electronic versions of printed books)

play audio and video files

keep a calendar and address book

do lots of other things using pieces of software that allow you to do things such as play games or draw cartoons

take photographs and make movies

Is cell phone radiation harmful?

Small amounts of the radio waves from cell phones go into the user's head. Some experts are worried about this. One study found that this low-level radiation could cause sleep problems. But another found that it could protect against Alzheimer's disease (a disease in which sufferers lose their memory) in later life. Health experts say there is no evidence of harm. But they encourage people not to use their cell phones too much. Long-term research will probably tell us much more about radiation and how much people are affected by cell phone use.

What does a SIM card do?

SIM stands for "Subscriber Identity Module." A **SIM card** is a portable memory chip. It has information about the personal details of a subscriber (the owner of the phone). The SIM card has two security passwords. There is a PIN (Personal Identification Number), which you type in to make the phone work. And there is a PUK (Personal Unblocking Key), which gets the SIM to work again if it has been locked. If you get your PIN wrong three times, your cell phone will lock you out. The PUK will let you in again. The SIM card contains all your personal information, including your phone book. You can take it out and put it into another phone to make it work for you.

The gold-colored memory chip of a SIM card sits in a piece of plastic. One corner of the plastic is cut off, so that it cannot be put in a phone the wrong way.

STANDARD AND MICRO

Some phones use a new, smaller card called a micro-SIM. This can also be used in a phone designed for the bigger, standard SIM. You just need a plastic adapter card.

Cell phone apps

Smartphones come with a number of **applications** (known as "apps") included. You can download more from the Internet. Apple has more than 200,000 apps for its iPhone. For students, there are a dictionary and thesaurus, measurement units converter, study notes, school schedule manager, and world atlas. For cooks, there are recipes, shopping lists, and conversion tables for ingredients. Or you might want to play games, such as Solitaire, Harry Potter: Spells, or Scrabble.

The smartphone attached to this bicycle uses an app of a compass. This shows the direction that the cyclist is traveling.

SHORT MESSAGE SERVICE

Are you part of the "thumb generation"? That is, are you a texter (a sender of text messages)? *SMS* stands for "Short Message Service." This service (used in cell phones and other devices) started in 1992 and has grown very fast since then. It has its own shorthand versions of words, such as *b4* for *before* and *CU* for *see you.*

Video, satellite, and cordless phones

Smartphones can use built-in cameras to send live video images across the world. This has done away with the need for separate **videophones**. Satellite phones are useful for journalists and emergency workers. They communicate with each other through satellites, rather than base stations. There are no base stations in far-off parts of the world, but satellites can always be used. Cordless phones are simply handsets that connect by radio to base stations plugged into land lines.

Cell phones can be very useful in an emergency. Climbers have even made calls from the top of the world's highest peak, Mount Everest.

SMS–SOS

On August 18, 2010, two British climbers were trapped in a storm 3,500 meters (11,480 feet) up the Italian Alps. Stuck on a ledge above a steep rock face, they could not move in the freezing conditions. They could not get through to emergency numbers on their cell phones. Both men's phone batteries were low, but they managed to text a friend in Shrewsbury, England—more than 1,000 kilometers (620 miles) away. They gave their location, the friend phoned the Italian emergency service, and a helicopter was able to lift them off the mountain.

E-WASTE

We all want the latest handheld gadgets. Models rarely last longer than a couple of years. Systems are upgraded, and new designs become available. But what do we do with our old computers and phones? The last thing we want to do is add to a mountain of electronic waste, or e-waste.

Think of the waste if we just throw away our old cell phones. If we really need a new phone, we should make sure the old one is reused or recycled.

What should we do?

Electronic devices contain **toxic** (poisonous) substances. They should never be thrown out with household trash. Many of the materials are recyclable. The device itself might be useful to someone else. So, there are three main ways of dealing with the problem:

- return the product to the manufacturer
- take it to a professional waste disposal facility
- donate it to a charity.

We should also ask ourselves the question: Do we really need the new model, or can we update the old one?

What could manufacturers do?

The environmental organization Greenpeace International says:

"Our three demands are that companies should:
- Clean up their products by eliminating hazardous [dangerous] substances
- Take back and recycle their products responsibly once they become obsolete [no longer usable]
- Reduce the climate [weather pattern] impacts of their operations and products."

Greenpeace also lists the greenest (least environmentally damaging) companies every year. You can look this up if you want to check how green your own gadgets are. (See page 46 for the web address.)

This is just a small part of a large pile of e-waste. If we deal with old gadgets sensibly, we can help the planet.

STAYING PRIVATE

Whatever you decide to do with your old computer, phone, or other gadget, you should first remove all your personal details. This means wiping all discs, drives, SIM cards, or other memory or storage devices. Remember to remove all address books and similar lists.

NAVIGATION ASSISTANTS

In recent years drivers, cyclists, hikers, and many other people have come to depend on satellite navigation (often shortened to **satnav**). Satnav acts like an electronic map to help people find their way. Like many other electronic devices, satnav receivers have become smaller, more powerful, and more useful. They all depend on the **Global Positioning System (GPS)** operated by the U.S. Air Force (see page 22). Russia, China, and the European Union are also working on new satellite systems.

GPS receivers

Personal navigation assistants (or PNAs) can be as small as a cell phone. Their basic function is to give users their location, which is shown as a position of **latitude** and **longitude**. These measurements tell us positions on Earth's surface (see "Coordinates," opposite). But today they are much more user-friendly. They show maps, so that you can see exactly where you are.

These hikers are using a GPS receiver to find their way. The device can show a map or give a list of instructions.

Satnav systems can also give spoken instructions. This is especially useful for drivers. Portable systems can be taken out of the car and used anywhere.

Coordinates

<u>Positions of latitude and longitude are called coordinates</u>. For example, the Empire State Building in New York is located at 40° 44′ 54.36″ N, 73° 59′ 08.36″ W. The first number is the latitude, given in degrees (°), minutes (′), and seconds (″) North. The second is the longitude in degrees West. The point where these coordinates cross is the precise location. On the other side of the world, Australia's Sydney Opera House is at 33° 51′ 25″ S, 151° 12′ 55″ E.

Use an atlas or a map to find out which famous landmarks are at:

a) 48° 85′ 83″ N, 2° 29′ 45″ E

b) 29° 58′ 45″ N, 31° 08′ 04″ E

c) 27° 10′ 27″ N, 78° 02′ 32″ E.

(Answers are on page 46.)

Desert rescue

In January 2009, a Romanian tourist got lost for six days in the central Australian desert. Luckily, he had a cell phone and a handheld GPS device with him. He called his family in Romania and gave them his exact position from the GPS. They called relatives in Melbourne, Australia, who contacted the police. He was found and rescued.

GLOBAL POSITIONING SYSTEM

The Global Positioning System (GPS) uses space satellites in orbit around Earth. The U.S. Air Force operates the 30 or so satellites that are currently working. Twenty-four are enough to give complete coverage of the planet. A GPS receiver on Earth needs information from at least three satellites to figure out its position.

The geometry of GPS

GPS works by geometry. That means, if you know how far you are from three other places, you can figure out where you are. In GPS, the three other places are satellites in space.

The U.S. space agency NASA launches rockets to carry satellites into space. The satellites send GPS information back to Earth.

DISTANCE AND THE SPEED OF LIGHT

Radio waves travel at the speed that light travels. That's about 300,000 kilometers (186,000 miles) per second! A GPS receiver figures out where a transmitting satellite is by timing how long its radio signal took to arrive. Its computer does a lot of complicated math!

How GPS works

Imagine you get lost in an unfamiliar country. First, you discover that you are 30 kilometers (19 miles) from village A. That means you could be anywhere on this circle, because every point on the circle is 30 kilometers from the center.

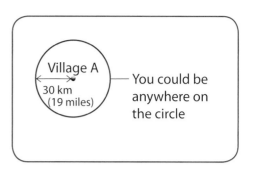

Then you learn that you are 50 kilometers (31 miles) from town B. This means you must be at one of the two points where the second circle meets the first. These are the only two spots that are 30 kilometers (19 miles) from A and 50 kilometers (31 miles) from B.

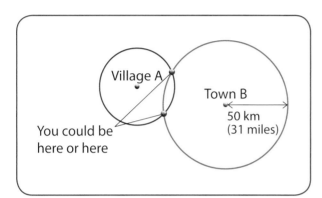

Third, you find out that you are 75 kilometers (47 miles) from city C. Now you know exactly where you are. You are at the point where all three circles cross each other.

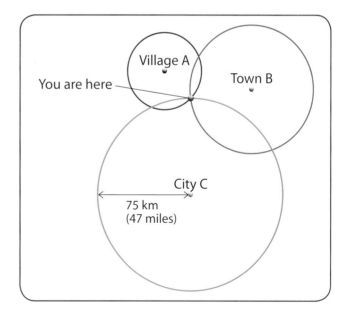

GPS works with spheres in three dimensions in space, instead of circles in two dimensions on paper. This makes the calculations more complicated, but the idea is the same.

Calculators

Pocket calculators first became available in the 1970s. They changed many people's way of working. For the first time, people could do complex arithmetic quickly and accurately. They could also take their calculator around with them.

Early calculators were expensive. In 1974 an early model cost around $175, which is the equivalent of around $750 today. A similar model today would cost less than $10. Even so, it would be more powerful than the early calculators were.

WHO DID THAT? ADDING AND SUBTRACTING

A French inventor named Louis Troncet developed a handheld mechanical calculator in 1889. His Arithmograph worked by moving rows of numbers with a metal pointer. Millions of these devices were sold.

In 1920 a German company started producing a machine called an Addiator. This did subtraction as well as addition. Later versions were still being produced in the 1980s.

More than 100,000 Addiators were sold in its first year.

What else can you "calculate"?

You can buy low-cost calculators that do lots of other things. Some calculators are also spellcheckers, crossword-puzzle solvers, and measurement converters. For example, they can quickly change feet into meters or degrees Fahrenheit into degrees Celsius. You can also buy handheld machines that include a dictionary, an encyclopaedia, a thesaurus, or a translator. One of these small machines can translate more than 200,000 words into six different languages.

A simple calculator like this can do all sorts of sums. It also has a memory, which makes it much easier to do big calculations.

solar panel

BRIGHT IDEA: SOLAR CELLS

You may have seen calculators with a solar panel at the top. The panel contains several **solar cells**. These are cells that power the device. The cells are **photovoltaic**. <u>Photovoltaic cells change sunlight into electricity</u>. They are also used in solar chargers, which power up rechargeable batteries in other handheld devices.

GAMES

The first computer games appeared in the 1970s. They had special cases called **cartridges** with computer disks in them. But these could do nothing else. Manufacturers soon realized that people wanted to play video games on the move. This led to handheld video game **consoles**, which were particularly popular with young people. At first the games were inserted on chunky cartridges. Today, they use slim game cards. A console called Wii has a handheld remote control for playing games on a separate screen.

Video game consoles are small and easy to carry.

NDS and PSP

Scientists, engineers, and designers sometimes come up with different ideas on how to make things easy or interesting for the gadget user. This happened with games machines. The two best-selling portable consoles came from Japan in 2004. The Nintendo DS has a dual screen (DS). The upper screen is the game monitor, and the lower is a touchscreen for entering commands. Sony's PlayStation Portable (PSP) has a single viewing screen with playing buttons to right and left.

In this game, players try to help alien creatures and robots save the galaxy from evil forces.

Walkthroughs

"Walkthroughs" can teach you how to complete and win video games. They are put together by experienced game players. Sometimes they are produced in the form of FAQs (Frequently Asked Questions). But for complicated games, they take (or walk) you through the game. These walkthroughs are sometimes called cheats. It is up to you to decide whether it is cheating if you use them.

FROM MICROVISION TO GAME BOY

The first handheld game console was Microvision, produced in 1979. It had cartridges for different games, but not very many. It was not a success. It was followed 10 years later by a hugely successful console: the Game Boy. It was just right for its time, with the latest games and a good, simple design. Nearly 119 million Game Boys were sold. The follow-up, Game Boy Advance, has sold another 81 million.

AUDIO

Until the 1990s, portable music players depended on separate physical storage such as records, tape cassettes, or CDs (compact discs). This changed when the first **digital audio players (DAPs)** were created in 1997. <u>The new DAPs store, organize, and play audio (sound) files on</u> **<u>hard-disk drives</u>** <u>or memory cards.</u> They are often called MP3 players, after the name of the system they use for storing and playing sound.

Engineers developed different designs for different companies. They also developed various ways of getting music onto the players. In 2001 Apple launched its iPod, which became the market leader in DAPs. In 2010 Apple said it had sold 250 million iPods.

These girls are sharing an MP3 player to enjoy music together. They are using earphones. But DAPs can also be put in a device called a dock and played through speakers.

PORTABLE MUSIC

The invention of the Sony Walkman in 1979 changed people's music-playing habits. This portable cassette player used headphones and was only slightly bigger than the cassette itself. It is said that the chairman of the Sony company wanted it developed so that he could listen to opera on long flights from Japan to the United States! Early models were called SoundAbout. But the name Walkman won out.

Downloading and piracy

Modern technology makes it possible for us to do all sorts of new things with our gadgets. But it is important that we are responsible in what we do. For example, technology now allows us to download songs to our music player from online stores, such as iTunes or Amazon. But there are other websites that allow illegal downloads (called **piracy**).

Illegal downloads break **copyright** laws, which give creative artists the right to control their own work and earn money from it. The Recording Industry Association of America says: "Plain and simple: piracy is bad news. While the term is commonly used, 'piracy' doesn't even begin to describe what is taking place. When you go online and download songs without permission, you are stealing … Artists, songwriters, musicians, record-company employees, and others in the industry all lose money."

E-READERS

The electronic-book reading device (or e-reader) was developed in the 1990s. Most models today are about the size of a hardback book, so that you see and read one page at a time. They have buttons or a touchscreen for turning pages and other commands.

Overtaking print?

In July 2010, the bookseller Amazon announced that in the previous three months it had sold more e-books than printed hardback books. In one month, the company sold 180 e-books for every 100 hardbacks. That shows how much technology is changing the way we read books.

Manufacturers say that their e-readers have a "no glare, paper-like display."

Pros and cons

The following are arguments in favor of the e-reader:

- It takes up less space than printed books.

- Its screen can be read in low light.

- An e-book never goes out of print.

- E-books are cheaper (although you have to buy the e-reader).

- E-books can be recovered if lost or damaged.

- They can be downloaded and read immediately.

- Printed books use three times more raw materials (paper and ink) to produce (without taking the e-reader into account).

The following are arguments against the e-reader:

- Individual e-books do not work on all readers.

- Not all printed books are available as e-books (some authors will not give their permission to do this*).

- E-books do not have the physical feel of a book cover and paper.

- E-books need batteries.

- You have to buy an e-reader before you read a book, and it could be lost or stolen.

- Customers cannot legally resell or lend their e-books to other readers.

- E-readers do not biodegrade (rot away), while paper is easily recycled.

HARRY POTTER

The author J. K. Rowling has not allowed her publisher to agree for her *Harry Potter* books to be published as e-books. In July 2010 her agent was reported as saying that she was considering changing her mind.

Cameras

The compact **digital** camera is the most popular camera today. By the turn of the 21st century, digital (computerized) technology was taking over from film photography. Since 1888 cameras had used special liquids to develop images from a thin strip of plastic (or film) and then make prints on paper. But digital cameras use an electronic process to capture images and save them on memory cards.

What are megapixels?

Digital cameras are often described in terms of how many megapixels they have. Pixels are tiny dots of light. Digital images are made up of millions of pixels. Megapixels measure resolution, which means the degree of detail visible in an image. The higher the number of megapixels, the more detail there is in an image.

More megapixels keep a picture sharp in close-up photography. This works if you enlarge a photograph, too, like this blow-up of the toucan's eye.

Point and shoot

Compact digital cameras are sometimes called "point-and-shoot" cameras. This is because the photographer does not need to adjust the camera in any way. It operates automatically. You just have to point it at your subject and press the button to take a photograph.

Live preview

The other advantage of digital cameras is "live preview." This means you can see exactly what you are photographing before you shoot, on an electronic display at the back of the camera. This is the same as the viewfinder on older cameras. You can also look at what you have just photographed instantly on the display. You can then decide to delete it or take another shot of the same subject. With film cameras, photographers had to wait to have the film developed to see their shots.

Point-and-shoot digital cameras take pictures without the need to adjust settings on the camera.

Instant cameras

During the second half of the 20th century, the Polaroid instant camera was very successful. This was a film camera that developed photographs very quickly, so that the photographer had an instant print. Digital cameras have replaced Polaroids for most purposes. But the Polaroid company has brought out a new instant digital camera. This is a digital camera with a built-in printer, so that you see your prints at once.

Early Polaroid cameras were bulky. They included the film packs for printing the photographs.

WHO DID THAT?
THE FIRST INSTANT CAMERA

Edwin Land (1909–91) was a U.S. scientist who invented the first instant camera. It was called the Polaroid Land camera. He founded the Polaroid Corporation in 1937 and produced his first instant camera with black-and-white film 10 years later. In 1963 Land added instant color film that developed within 50 seconds. The Polaroid was the best-known instant film camera.

Making movies

Earlier camera recorders (or camcorders) used video tape. But digital camcorders record on an internal memory called a hard-disk drive. They store hours of film material, which can easily be transferred to a computer or watched on a TV screen. Most compact digital cameras shoot movies as well as still images. They can be watched on the camera's monitor or transferred to a computer.

Compact digital camcorders are small and light. This makes them easy to use while on vacation.

YOU CAN BE A SPY!

Now you can buy a ballpoint pen that has a built-in digital video camera with a microphone and a memory stick. The pen records for about 1 hour from one charge of the battery. It can store 15 hours of video and sound. The pen fits neatly into a jacket or shirt pocket. Advertisers say that the pen is perfect for undercover journalists and private investigators. What they really mean is it is perfect for spying. This gadget may be fun, but some people would think that it invades their privacy.

SCANNERS

In the science fiction TV and movie series *Star Trek*, characters use a handheld gadget called a tricorder. It scans data and machinery, and it is used for medical purposes, too. This must have seemed incredible to viewers when the series started in 1966.

Today, various gadgets, including smartphones, can achieve the same results as the fictional tricorder. Medical scanners are able to look inside a patient's body without doing any harm. Metal detectors help people search for ancient coins and other metal objects. Image scanners are used to reproduce pictures or documents.

Ultra-scanner

In 2010 an international health care company launched a handheld **ultrasound scanner**. This is a device that sends out sound waves. The sound waves bounce off internal body parts such as the heart. The scanner creates images from the waves that bounce back. The new flip-top scanner has a separate instrument that is held against the patient's body.

Ultrasound scanners are used regularly when pregnant women go for checkups.

Scanning apps

There are many apps available to turn smartphones into medical scanners. More and more doctors are using them, but some have not yet been approved by the world's medical authorities. They want the phones to be tested more, so that they can be certain they are reliable.

In 2010 a researcher in London, England, developed an app that turns a phone into a stethoscope for listening to a patient's breathing and heartbeat. There is even an app that asks patients to cough into their phone. It then tells them if they have the flu, pneumonia, or another illness.

DETECTING GOLD

On July 5, 2009, Terry Herbert's metal detector helped him discover small objects beneath a plowed field in central England. The objects were gold. Eventually more than 1,500 pieces were recovered. Experts said that they were about 1,400 years old. The sword fittings, crosses, and decorative items were cleaned and cataloged at the British Museum. They were valued at just under $5 million. Herbert and the owner of the farmland shared the reward between them.

These are just some of the gold objects found by Terry Herbert. His discoveries made him a wealthy man.

Security wands

Security wands are used at airports and other places to scan passengers for metal objects, especially weapons. The wand is really just a small metal detector. A security officer waves the wand close to the passenger's body. The wand either bleeps or lights up to show that metal is nearby. Some police officers use silent versions that give a vibrating signal. This means that they are aware of the metal and can take action without alerting the person carrying the suspicious object.

This security wand is being used at the World Athletics Championships in Finland in 2005.

Barcode readers

Barcodes are patterns of vertical lines and numbers that identify an item and often its price. You will find one on the back of this book, showing its unique International Standard Book Number (ISBN). Handheld readers can decode the lines. This helps identify the book, so that it is stored in the right place.

Barcode scanners

Barcodes also make it easy to count the amount of a particular book in stock. This can be useful in warehouses, bookstores, and libraries. People who work there can use a scanner to read the barcode, just as they do with goods in a supermarket.

Pointing the finger

Have you ever seen your own fingerprints? If you have, you will know that the most amazing thing about fingerprints is that every finger is different. And everyone has a completely different set of fingerprints. Each one is unique. That makes fingerprints ideal for security devices. Fingerprint scanners can be separate or built into another gadget, such as a computer mouse. The scanner takes a digital image of your index finger. This can then be used to allow entry to a computer, certain programs, or even your front door. You put your finger on the reader, and the reader scans it. If it matches the original, it allows you to move on. Your fingerprint is your password.

The police officer is scanning a person's fingerprint. The scan can be stored and used as evidence if fingerprints are found at a crime scene.

REMOTE CONTROL

The kind of TV remote control we use today was launched in the 1970s. It changed many people's viewing habits. Viewers liked being able to change channels without having to walk over to the TV set. It was not long before similar remote controls came in for stereos and other equipment.

Infrared signals

Most television remote controls work by **infrared** radiation. These rays have greater energy than radio waves (see page 5). When you point the device at your TV and press a button, it sends an infrared beam to a receiver in the TV. The receiver decodes the infrared information. It changes it into an electrical signal to change the TV settings.

The remote control is a familiar device in many homes now.

Into the future

The range and power of handheld gadgets have changed dramatically since 2000. Many of them, such as the latest smartphones, are really miniature computers with giant power. They allow us to keep in touch with each other through email, text message, and networking services. Many of the gadgets described in this book have helped create a revolution in communication. Will this continue in the future, with even newer ways of communicating? Or will future handheld gadgets have other uses that we are not even aware of yet?

MYSTERY CONTROL

"Most thrilling invention since radio itself! No wires. No plug-in. No cords of any kind! It's truly unbelievable! It's mystifying! That's why it's called Mystery Control!" This was how Philco advertised its wireless Mystery Control radio remote in 1939. It was the first handheld gadget of its kind. It was made of wood and very chunky. You could change channels and alter volume with it, all from the comfort of your armchair. It used radio waves, not infrared like today's remote controls.

Other instruments we use today work like our handheld gadgets. This is a touchscreen dashboard in a car.

KEEPING SAFE

Gadgets can do amazing things, but things can go wrong.
Here are some tips to help you keep your cell phone
and computer systems safe.

- Always back up your data on an external hard drive, CD, memory stick, or other device. Ask an adult for help with this if you need it.

- Always use passwords, but avoid choosing obvious words or always using the same one.

- Install security software that protects against viruses (see page 11), spyware, and spam (junk e-mail). Never open an email attachment that is in any way suspicious.

Identity theft

Your personal information is very useful to an identity thief, who
can use your details by pretending to be you. Never give details
to unauthorized people. If you suspect that someone is trying to
get information—such as user names, passwords, or other details
from you—do not reply. Report it to a trusted authority. (This
attempt to get your details is called phishing.)

- When checking emails: If in doubt, throw it out.

- When online: If in doubt, log out.

Quick Quiz

Try this quiz to see what you have learned about handheld gadgets. Then turn to page 46 for the answers.

1. Which of these waves and rays have the least energy?

a) X-rays

b) microwaves

c) radio waves

d) infrared rays

2. What does SIM stand for?

a) security instant memory

b) safe install mouse

c) smartphone input modem

d) subscriber identity module

3. What should you NOT do with an old electronic gadget?

a) give it to a charity

b) throw it away

c) take it to a waste disposal facility

d) return it to the manufacturer

4. How fast do radio waves travel?

a) 300,000 kilometers (186,000 miles) per hour

b) 300,000 kilometers (186,000 miles) per minute

c) 300,000 kilometers (186,000 miles) per second

d) 300 kilometers (186,000 miles) per second

5. What kind of energy do photovoltaic cells use?

a) wind

b) nuclear

c) biomass

d) solar

6. What is image resolution measured in?

a) megapixels

b) megabytes

c) megabucks

d) megahertz

7. Who invented the instant camera?

a) George Eastman

b) Edwin Fuji

c) Edwin Land

d) Peter Polaroid

8. What is a security wand used for?

a) detecting paper money

b) finding treasure

c) setting a password

d) detecting metal

Glossary

antenna device that receives and transmits radio signals

application (or **app**) computer program that performs a specific task

attachment file added to an email message

backup make extra copies of something in case the original is lost

base station place in a cell that receives and sends cell phone signals

browser computer program that helps you search for things on the World Wide Web

cartridge container holding computer disks—for example, for playing computer games

cell area around a base station that receives and sends cell phone signals

charge amount of electricity

component part of something, such as part of a gadget

console device with a set of controls—for example, for playing computer games

copyright legal right of creative artists to control their own work and earn money from it

cursor movable pointer on a computer screen

data information

digital device that processes information in digits (numbers)

digital assistant electronic personal organizer with a calendar, address book, and other features

digital audio player (DAP) device that stores, organizes, and plays audio (sound) files on hard-disk drives or memory cards. DAPS are often called MP3 players.

electromagnetic relating to electricity and magnetism, especially in energy from the Sun

energy ability to do work

frequency rate at which vibrations occur in a wave, such as a radio wave

Global Positioning System (GPS) system that tracks the exact position of a person or vehicle using a system of satellites

hard-disk drive device that allows a computer or another electronic gadget to store information on a rigid disk

hotspot area where computers can use a wireless network to connect to the Internet

hyperlink link from one part of a document to another that works by clicking on it or touching it

infrared referring to a kind of radiation that has greater energy than radio waves

latitude imaginary line running around Earth, showing the distance north or south of the equator

longitude imaginary line running up and down the Earth from the North to the South Pole, showing the distance east or west of Greenwich, England

microchip small component that makes electronic gadgets work

mouse device that allows you to move a computer cursor, choose options, and give instructions

photovoltaic producing electricity from sunlight, as in a solar cell

piracy illegally copying copyrighted material

portable designed to be easily carried around

radiation range of electrical and magnetic rays given off by the Sun, including radio waves

radio wave electromagnetic wave of energy that is useful for long-distance communication

receiver device that picks up radio signals

router device that connects individual computers to the Internet

satellite object that orbits Earth in space and can receive and send signals

satnav short for "satellite navigation," it is a device that acts like an electronic map to help people find their way

service provider company that connects people and their computers to the Internet

SIM card portable memory chip that contains a cell phone owner's personal details

smartphone cell phone that has functions that allow you to use it as a computer

software computer programs that give instructions to make a computer perform tasks

solar cell device that turns sunlight into electricity

tablet computer small computer with a touchscreen

touchpad small panel on a computer that acts like a mouse and allows you to move a cursor and choose options

touchscreen screen that shows options that you choose by touching them with your finger

toxic poisonous or very harmful

transistor small component that makes electronic gadgets work

transmitter device that sends radio signals

ultrasound scanner device that uses high-frequency sound waves to create images

videophone telephone that sends and receives pictures as well as sound

virus in computing, a program that can spread from one device to another and damage or destroy information

walkie-talkie portable two-way radio transmitter and receiver

Wi-Fi wireless connection used to access the Internet

World Wide Web enormous set of documents contained in websites and pages on the Internet

Find Out More

Books

Hile, Lori. *Mastering Media: Social Networks and Blogs.* Chicago: Raintree, 2011.

Morris, Neil. *From Fail to Win!: Gadgets and Inventions.* Chicago: Raintree, 2011.

Oxlade, Chris. *Tales of Invention: The Computer.* Chicago: Heinemann Library, 2011.

Throp, Claire. *Culture in Action: Digital Music: A Revolution in Music.* Chicago: Raintree, 2011.

Websites

How Stuff Works
www.howstuffworks.com
This website explains … well, how stuff works. The web pages are written in simple language. They include information on all sorts of gadgets and are kept up-to-date.

Greenpeace International
www.greenpeace.org/international/campaigns/toxics/electronics
Greenpeace provides information about "greener electronics" and offers solutions to businesses and consumers.

Computer Science Lab
www.computersciencelab.com/ComputerHistory/History.htm
This has an illustrated history of computers, with lots of fascinating photographs.

Answers to quizzes

Page 21: a) Eiffel Tower, Paris, France; b) Great Pyramid, Giza, Egypt; c) Taj Mahal, Agra, India.

Page 43: 1 (c), **2** (d), **3** (b), **4** (c), **5** (d), **6** (a), **7** (c), **8** (d).

Topics to investigate

There are many different topics related to handheld gadgets. The websites on page 46 might give some interesting leads. Here are some more research ideas.

Looking back

Imagine what life must have been like in 1950, well before the age of the personal computer and cell phone. There were not even any pocket calculators. What were the differences in communication? Did people use different forms of communication—written letters, for example? Put "1950s life" into an Internet search engine, and you will find lots of websites to get you started.

Looking forward

What will be the most useful, most fun handheld gadgets in 2050? Will they be very different from the ones mentioned in this book? No one knows, but you can make a guess. Do you think gadgets will continue to get smaller? Or is there a point when they are too small to be useful? Make a list of gadgets you would like to see developed. Maybe you could design one or two yourself.

Science

You could research the science behind electronic gadgets. There is some information on the electromagnetic spectrum on page 5 in this book. Put the term into an Internet search engine. There is lots more information for you to look at. You could also do more research on electricity.

Security

Security is a serious issue, and you could do more research on issues such as identity theft. What are the dos and don'ts on the Internet?

Index